A LAKELAND CAMERA

Yesterday's industry: the charcoal burner

A LAKELAND CAMERA

DAVID JONES

MICHAEL RUSSELL

For my wife Mavis

I should like to thank the many people who gave up their valuable time to assist me in compiling this book. Without their help and cooperation the task would have been impossible.

Grange-over-Sands 1980 DAVID JONES

First published in Great Britain 1980
by Michael Russell (Publishing) Ltd,
The Chantry, Wilton, Salisbury

Printed in Great Britain
by Biddles Ltd., Guildford, Surrey

ISBN 0 85955 080 X

ABOVE: Marking hounds at the start of a hound trail, Cartmel Show. They are first counted and then marked on shoulder or head with a soft crayon.

RIGHT: The trail is laid by licensed trailers (who are paid officials), dragging a mixture of aniseed, paraffin, turpentine and oil on a rag. The scent will be strongest at the start of a trail because there are two trailers starting from a central point, one walking towards the start, one towards the finish; so the scent at the. start will have had the least time to fade.

'The slip' at Lowick Show. The trailer has come in, the starter's flag has dropped and away go the hounds over the fells.

ABOVE: The start. Racing past the trailer.

BELOW: Up and over. Hounds at Eskdale Show.

Owners and trainers urging on their hounds for a final effort. The trail is shortened in hot weather and lengthened for rain, and in hot weather more oil is added to the trailer's rag to hold down the scent. On average the ground covered by a trailer in one hour of fast walking is covered by a hound in ten minutes. There is a maximum time of forty-five minutes for a senior or old dogs' trail and a minimum of twenty-five minutes. If these times are not adhered to, the trail is null and void. For a puppy these times would be reduced to twenty-five and fifteen minutes. Officials keep watch at crossings and other key points to ensure safety and fair play, and all trails and hounds are controlled and registered by the Hound Trailing Association. Each puppy has a number punched in one ear, rather like a tattoo, and the year of birth is punched in the other. At the start of each trail the judge can check if the hound is registered.

ABOVE: The moment of victory for hound and trainer at Lowick Show. The hound is looking eagerly at the contents of the bowl in the trainer's hand – it will be twenty-four hours since it had its last feed. Food given to the hound in the final days before a race is designed to keep it cool and consists mainly of white meat such as chicken. Cutting the hound's coat very short is also reckoned to help, a process known as 'clipping out'.

A hound is at its peak when three years old. The first year it runs as a puppy, the second it runs with the older dogs, usually lacking their stamina and experience. It is a very good dog that wins the championship twice, though there have been those who won it three times.

RIGHT: Greetings for the trainer after a trail at Wasdale Show.

RIGHT: Fred Reeves breasts the tape to win the fell race at Ambleside Sports. In his right hand is the tag which runners have to collect at the top of the climb to prove they have completed the full course. Fred Reeves and his rival Tom Sedgewick were the outstanding Lakeland fell runners of the 1970s. Reeves won the Senior Guides Race at Grasmere in 1969 at his first attempt (a feat not accomplished in 121 years), and in 1974 went on to beat the famous Bill Teasdale's record for Grasmere which was set up in 1965. Tom Sedgewick took the record off him two years later, but Reeves regained it in 1978, the season in which he was undefeated in all his thirty-one races.

BELOW: Colin Lightfoot winning the Junior Guides Race at Ambleside Sports. His father stands ready to welcome him, while holding the tape is Bill Teasdale of Caldbeck.

The Senior Guides Race at Grasmere Sports. The competitors race up the fell and round Castle Rock before making a spectacular return down the steep fell side to the sports field.

The mummers' play celebrating the rebirth of Nature in spring takes place at 'Pace Egging' or Easter. The Furness Morris Men are here performing on Easter Monday in the square at Cartmel. Each actor presents a distinctive character in unusual attire: (ABOVE) in procession come The Doctor, Tosspot, Old Beelzebub, Betty Askett and the Prince of Paradise singing 'Here come two or three jolly boys all in a row'. The play centres on a duel between The Prince of Paradise and St George, seen (LEFT) issuing his challenge. His blackened face is to ensure that he is not recognised before the performance, for this would break the luck.

OPPOSITE, ABOVE: The duel takes place and the Prince of Paradise is defeated, falling to the ground. The Doctor has the answer. 'A drop of this sip sap' (i.e. rum) revives the Prince (OPPOSITE, BELOW).

Mrs Rosemary Graham and her mother-in-law make all the butter that the family uses at Wythop Hall Farm. In summer the separated milk from their Friesian cows is left for a week before being put into the churn. In winter it takes two weeks. Water is added to the cream in the churn, which is then turned by the tractor motor. After this, the butter is washed, salted and weighed into pounds. Then it is patted into 'loaves' and placed on the slate to cool. The best butter is made in summer when the cows are out at grass; the Grahams store it for the winter in their deep freeze.

ABOVE: Mrs Graham senior taking the butter from the churn.

LEFT: The butter is made ready for weighing.

OPPOSITE, ABOVE: The butter is weighed into pounds.

OPPOSITE, BELOW: Rosemary Graham pats the butter into shape.

CEYLON

Charcoal was originally produced in quantity in the Lake District for iron and gunpowder manufacturers. Traditional production methods did not provide a sufficiently refined substance for the quarrying industry's gunpowder, so their charcoal came to be produced by the retort method instead. The iron industry gradually abandoned charcoal for coke, though the Backbarrow Iron Furnace was converted to coke only in 1926. Locally, charcoal burning survived a little longer – the Ellwood family of Oxen Park were making high quality charcoal well into the 1930s for use in domestic irons.

In the summer of 1972 Jack Allonby of Spark Bridge near Greenodd, together with Bill Norris, re-enacted a charcoal burn under the eye of Jack's 83-year-old uncle, Tyson Allonby of Bouth, who had spent much of his working life as a charcoal burner.

LEFT, ABOVE: The stack is constructed of wood around a single central pole, with a covering of reeds or dried grass topped with fine sandy soil (except for the top, where turf is used). The central pole is cut down and a pointed piece of timber is inserted called a 'motty peg'. This is removed when the stack is lit.

LEFT, BELOW: Bill Norris brings glowing charcoal in a pan. The charcoal is put in the hole left by the removal of the 'motty peg', then a layer of turf seals the stack. There is therefore not sufficient air for the wood to ignite, so the stack smoulders and slowly chars the wood. It is possible to gauge the rate of burn by the movement of a dark band of moisture and tars which moves down the dome as the burn progresses.

OPPOSITE, ABOVE: The stack is smouldering. Jack Allonby checks that all is well before sealing the hole. A barrel of water stands nearby for dousing the stack.

OPPOSITE, BELOW: A day and a half has passed. Jack Allonby is making good a cavity that has appeared in the stack. A burn lasts approximately three days.

ABOVE: Harry Baines, of Backbarrow near Newby Bridge, seated in the woods of the Winster Valley making besoms. The cuttings, or 'chats', are taken from a young birch tree during the winter months. The dry 'chats' are chopped down to yard-long pieces and then placed in the tight grasp of the 'besom engine', specially made at Allithwaite smithy. The 'spinner' wraps wire round the ends – in years gone by cane was used instead of wire and the besom heads were often sent away to have the handles attached. Here Harry Baine's son George inserts the handle and the besom is completed.

OPPOSITE, ABOVE: George Baines trims the head of the 'chats' with an axe.

OPPOSITE, BELOW: George Baines inserts the handle into the tightly bound besom head and with a few strong blows ensures the shaft is secure. Besom handles are made of ash or hazel.

RIGHT: Coniston Foxhounds setting off for the first draw at the Troutbeck Mayor's Hunt.

FAR RIGHT, ABOVE: Huntsman Anthony Chapman, whose father was huntsman before him, yells instructions to his hounds – one of whom, Cragsman (FAR RIGHT, BELOW), finds time during the hunt to pose for the camera. Anthony Chapman, a farmer, started with the Coniston Foxhounds in 1932 as whipper in and became huntsman in 1944.

BELOW: Anthony Chapman leads the hunt across a bridge in the Winster Valley at the start of a day. The Lakeland Fell Packs, as they are known, hunt on foot, the terrain being generally too rough for horses.

ABOVE and OPPOSITE, ABOVE: Hounds on the move in otter hunting days. Huntsman Tom Harrison leads the Kendal and District pack alongside the River Mint and then takes hounds across the water.

RIGHT: Beagles moving off at the start of a day. The Lake District has several packs of beagles and harriers, and packs from other parts of the country also visit the area.

ABOVE: Farrier Sam Eakins, a regular at Appleby Horse Fair for nearly twenty years, has his home in the Midlands but lives with the fair for these hectic days. Horse trading takes place during the whole of Fair Week, but on the second Wednesday in June the horse sale begins in earnest. Up on Fair Hill the young people enjoy putting the animals through their paces along the campside road. A clap of hands between buyer and seller seals the bargain. The fair has developed into a major trading and social event for the travelling people.

OPPOSITE, ABOVE: Another regular at the Horse Fair is fortune teller Gypsy Caroline Lee, seen here in the family caravan. The traditional gypsy's feeling for colour and decoration plays its part in this busy interior.

OPPOSITE, BELOW: A decorated cart, adapted for passenger use, is driven past the lines of caravans on the encampment.

Washing the horses in the River Eden has become almost a ritual. The horses are given a good coating of washing-up liquid and then ridden bareback into the water.

This magnificent example of a gypsy caravan was to be seen at the 1978 fair. The caravan was originally the home of Mrs Jane Dorothy Smith of Doncaster (who raised a family of eleven children) and the restoration work was carried out by John Pickett of Berwick St John in Wiltshire. Two visitors to the fair pose at the entrance, while behind the no-nonsense figure on the right may be seen the new-style gypsy caravan with its somewhat less artistic embellishments of chrome. On seeing one of the modern caravan interiors, one visitor likened it to travelling in a crystal ball. Which, if you happen to be Gypsy Caroline Lee, is after all not too inappropriate.

An impromptu concert on Fair Hill Field.

In 1412 Henry IV gave a charter to his youngest son, Thomas of Lancaster, entitling him and his heirs to hold a market in his manor at Flookburgh every Tuesday and also to hold two annual fairs. Charles II confirmed the charter and the manuscript is preserved in the church of St John the Baptist. In 1950 the Rev. Charles Fowler initiated an annual ceremony for the reading of the charter. A Charter Queen is chosen in June and after she has walked in procession (OPPOSITE, ABOVE) and been crowned in the square, she reads aloud from the decorated scroll of vellum bearing in one corner a small portrait of Charles II. ABOVE, Karen Linklater sits on her throne after reading the charter. The Flookburgh Silver Band (OPPOSITE, BELOW) turns out for the occasion and there is a fancy dress parade.

Visitors to the Lake District usually have their first view of Cumberland and Westmorland wrestling at the famous Grasmere Sports. The contest is heralded by the ringing of a bell and the calling of the contestant's name three times before the shaking of hands. If the wrestler does not appear, he is disqualified – this is known as being 'blawn out'. After the prizes for skill at the sport there are awards for the best costume. All contestants wear long white tights and vests with trunks with a plush 'seat piece', though for displays specially embroidered or decorated trunks may be worn.

ABOVE: In this match at Grasmere Sports the wrestler on the left is winning a fall with a right-legged 'hipe'. The 'hipe', which has many variations, is a move which basically relies on lifting one leg high to trip and swing the opponent while the other is placed between the opponent's legs to unbalance him.

OPPOSITE, ABOVE: 'Taking hod': the wrestlers rest their head on each other's shoulder, clasp their hands behind each other's back, and the contest proper begins.

OPPOSITE, BELOW: The wrestlers crash to the ground in a tangle of arms and legs. The wrestler on top won this fall with a 'cross buttock'.

J. Robinson of Park End Farm, Underbarrow, holding the belt won by his great-grandfather at Crosthwaite Sports' wrestling, 20 September 1833.

OPPOSITE, BELOW: The winners of the Best Wrestlers' Costume Competition at Grasmere Sports.

ABOVE: J. Strong, of Caldbeck, one of Lakeland's last remaining clog makers.

ABOVE: Fell Foot Farm, at the foot of Wrynose Pass, has particular connections with Lanty Slee, the celebrated nineteenth-century smuggler who distilled a potent spirit from potato peelings. This illicit brew was stored occasionally at Fell Foot, a seventeenth-century building with a sixteenth-century north wing. The barn is attached to the house, with the local slate left bare – unlike the house itself, which is roughcast and limewashed. The projecting feature above the doorway may originally have been a small spinning gallery.

OPPOSITE, ABOVE: Joe Fawcett sits beside his handsome old-fashioned kitchen range at Glassonby, near Penrith. Built by J. Altham of Penrith, it has a side boiler and an oven on the left in which Ada Fawcett would cook the Christmas goose. The 'tidy betty' is at the bottom of the fireplace.
OPPOSITE, BELOW: One of the bedrooms of Townend, Troutbeck, a fine example of a statesman's house. Built in 1623, Townend was the home of the Browne family without a break until 1944. It is now owned by the National Trust.

Farmer George Birkett (ABOVE) lives in Little Langdale in probably the oldest house in the dale – Birk Howe Farm (OPPOSITE, BELOW), now owned by the National Trust. It is sixteenth century with a seventeenth-century addition (on the left of the photograph). The farm embodies many of the traditional features of a statesman's house, with its long low line, porches and dripstones. The central chimney has an oval shaft. Inside there is a semi-spiral stone staircase.

OPPOSITE, ABOVE: The seventeenth-century ramp barn at Townend, Troutbeck, is perhaps the finest surviving example, with galleries not unlike spinning galleries on either side of the ramp. The projecting wings are thought to have housed farm labourers. These ramp barns are quite common in Lakeland: they are built of stone with a slate roof and are of two stories. The lower usually has cattle stalls, with the barn on the upper floor.

ABOVE: A farmer in his 'Sunday best' concentrates on one of the sights at Eskdale Show.

LEFT, ABOVE: Team effort in the tug o' war – always a popular event at Rusland Sports.

LEFT, BELOW: Rusland Sports, and the end of the road for the anchor man in one of the defeated tug o' war teams.

ABOVE: Judging the foxhounds at Mellbreak Show. These handlers walk the hounds for the various Fell Packs during the summer months.

LEFT: A young Herdwick tup at Lowick Show.

OPPOSITE, ABOVE: Enjoying a joke at Rydal Show.

OPPOSITE, BELOW: Two young girls doing battle at Eskdale Show.

ABOVE: Visitors at Cartmel Show studying an exhibit of mangolds.

OPPOSITE, ABOVE: Denis Barrow, huntsman of the Ullswater Foxhounds, with a silver salver at Loweswater Show. The competition is for 'the best dressed huntsman, with a couple of hounds and a couple of terriers'.

OPPOSITE, BELOW: Wasdale Show, Best Shepherd's Dog Competition.

Two terrier owners at Mellbreak Show keep a watchful eye on a slightly unpredictable interview.

A competitor in the horn blowing competition at the Eskdale and Ennerdale Foxhounds Show.

ABOVE: At Eskdale Show Stan Edmonson of Seathwaite, Borrowdale examines the wool of a Herdwick before deciding which animal will be overall show champion. The hill farmers round the show ring doubtless have their own ideas.

RIGHT: Joe Wear, retired huntsman of Ullswater Foxhounds, judging foxhounds at Eskdale Show.

OPPOSITE: Best Shepherd's Dog Competition at Eskdale Show, with Hardknott in the background.

Although as a product it is now seriously in decline, the success of the swill has always been in its practical shape and its strength. It is made in three parts – the hazel rim or 'bool', the main framework of wider oak strips and the narrow oak strips which are interwoven and are known as 'taws'. A good craftsman would make approximately 25 to 30 swills in a week, and this includes the preparation of the wood as well as the actual weaving. Sadly, there are few young craftsmen coming to take the places of the older men.

RIGHT: Before being incorporated in the basket, each piece of oak has much of the roughness removed with a knife.

BELOW: Slender pieces of hazel coppice are boiled for a short time to make them more pliable and then bent into an oval-shaped rim with the aid of this special machine.

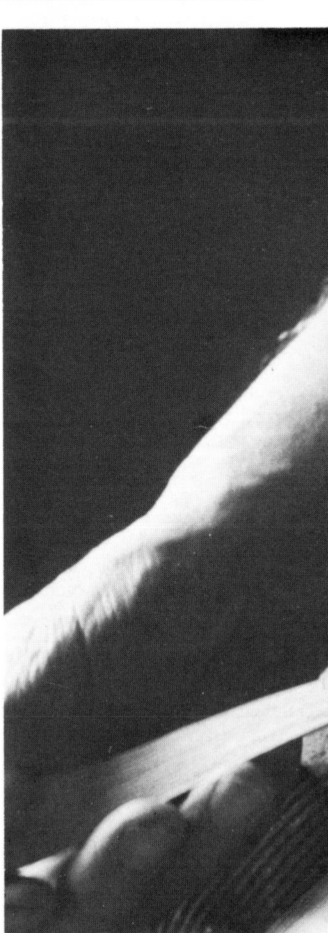

LEFT: The shape of the swill is governed by the firm but even pressure exerted as the basket is woven. Here the strips are in position and the taws are being woven.

BELOW: The 'central lapping' strip has turned down strips on either side. The craftsman secures the end of this most important strip by folding it back over the hazel rim and weaving a knot taw. Other strips do not overlap the rim but are inserted into a slit made in the rim with a bodkin.

'Ligging' or 'splashing' a 'dyke' is a local Lakeland term for laying or dressing a hedge. The ideal time to do this is when the sap stops running in October; with only short breaks during the heavy frosts, conditions are suitable until March. An older hedge is better laid in spring, when the sap starts to rise and the wood, which otherwise might snap, becomes more pliable.

Fred Coward (ABOVE), of Lindale, prefers to lay his hedges at intervals of roughly nine to ten years. For the first three years after laying the hedge should be topped; after that, allowed to grow for six to seven years. Hawthorn or blackthorn are ideal, since they provide a stock-proof fence which grows dense and low and offers little temptation to the stock for grazing. A typical hedge in southern Lakeland is grown on top of a bank of turf and stone.

ABOVE: The hedger slices the base of each stem of wood with a long tapering cut, made as low as possible on the branch; then he bends or 'lays' the branch horizontally, and cuts off any tongue of wood from the stump, encouraging new wood to grow from the base, and thickening the hedge. All this new growth is subsequently woven along the horizontal line of the cut branches. This is called 'raddling the brush' (OPPOSITE, ABOVE). It is wise to wear thick thorn-proof gauntlets when dealing with blackthorn and a peaked cap helps to ward thorns from the eyes. Stout stakes hold the 'brush' in place (OPPOSITE, BELOW); by the time they are rotten, the hedge will have grown naturally into the hedger's mould. A strand of barbed wire, about four feet from the ground and nailed to the stakes, gives some protection against stock for the first couple of years of the hedge's life.

A farm disposal sale at Low Green Farm, Lindale. Auctioneer George Lawrence prises bids from a thoughtful audience.

Ron Thompson, driver of *Bertha,* the Levens Hall Fowler Showman's Road Locomotive, at the Beetham Vintage Ploughing Competition.

ABOVE: *Lakeland Princess,* a 1914 Marshall steam roller, winner of the Supreme Award for traction engines at the sixth annual Cumbria Steam Gathering in 1978. It spent all its working life at Penrith, and was bought in 1968 by Dick Ransome, of Torver near Coniston. He spent seven years restoring the engine to its former glory – which included building a new smokebox, water tank and coal bunker and retubing the boiler.

BELOW: 'The Most Popular Riding Machine' is a Steam Galloper owned by Mrs Ayres of Southall, Middlesex, and operated by her husband Frank. The Galloper, which also has an organ, is thought to be about sixty years old, one of only four travelling machines of this kind. The helter skelter on the left is the only surviving travelling one in the country. It is known as a 'slip' in showman's slang and is thought to be seventy-five years old.

ABOVE: The wet dock at Windermere Steamboat Museum. In the foreground is the steam launch *Otto,* built in 1896. She has a speed of 18 m.p.h. The steam launch *Lady Elizabeth* (centre) was salvaged off Bowness and is typical of the launches used for fishing for char on Lake Windermere. On the right is steam launch *Dolly,* listed in the *Guinness Book of Records* as the oldest mechanically powered boat in the world. Built in about 1850 at Windermere, she was discovered by divers in 1960 on the bed of Ullswater, having sunk in the winter of 1895. She was salvaged and brought back to Windermere to be slowly dried out and restored to her present condition.

RIGHT, ABOVE: The private steam launch *Branksome* on Lake Windermere. Built locally in 1896, she has a side-fired locomotive-type boiler, a fifty-foot carvel teak hull, and a speed of 14 m.p.h.

RIGHT, BELOW: Locomotive *Repulse,* a Hunslet Austerity 0-6-0, prepares to haul the 1.55 p.m. the three-and-a-half miles from Haverthwaite to Lake Side. The local railway was opened in 1869, closed for passenger traffic in 1965, but this section was reopened in 1973 for the summer months.

Although the peeling of bark is associated mainly with tanneries, the by-product of stripped oak is made into rustic furniture. Only oak provides the tannin-yielding bark used in the production of fine quality leather, but few tanneries can now afford traditional lengthy processes and the bark peeler is a disappearing species, having to follow other woodland trades to augment his income. Jack Allonby (ABOVE and OPPOSITE, ABOVE), here at work in the woods near Ickenthwaite in the Rusland Valley, has been a coppice woodman for over forty years, following both his father and his grandfather. Another bark peeler (OPPOSITE, BELOW) is Chris Malone, also of Spark Bridge near Greenodd, seen peeling oak coppice.

The bark peeler would expect to buy the standing wood and set about cutting the oak as the sap began to rise in mid April or May. After the bark has been peeled with a special knife, it is stacked (ABOVE) in the open to dry. About seven tons of wood will produce one ton of bark, which is ground for tanning purposes and layered between hides.

The remains of a bark peeler's hut in the woods near Coniston Water.
The woodman and his family would live here during the summer months.

Since the production of snuff is basically a grinding process, the siting of mills tended to be where there was water power readily available. The Kendal area, with the fast-flowing River Kent and its tributaries, was an ideal centre and the industry was first established there in 1792 when Thomas Harrison brought from Scotland some grinding machinery and a formula for making snuff. His daughter eloped with a Samuel Gawith; and one of their six sons married the sister of Henry Hoggarth – which is how the firm acquired its present name of Gawith Hoggarth & Co Ltd. Its mill at Helsington on the River Kent (ABOVE) is powered solely by the water wheel. It has been calculated that this produces approximately 6 b.h.p.

The tobacco leaf is imported principally from East Africa, the United States, Malawi, India and Canada. There are two kinds of snuff, dry working and wet working. The leaf for dry working is dried on the floor of a heated drying room in an outbuilding. At the next stage, in the mill itself, it is enclosed in a drum and crushed into powder by steel balls. The wet worked snuff is placed in four wooden mortars with revolving steel pestles, until it has reached the correct consistency and is moist enough. The ground tobacco is scooped out, transferred to a three-pestle mortar, then mixed in a pot with inorganic salt. Finally the ground snuff is sifted to the appropriate consistency according to the type required.

OPPOSITE, ABOVE: Les Metcalf, the foreman at Gawith Hoggarth's mill at Helsington, inspecting the tobacco leaf prior to the first grinding process.

OPPOSITE, BELOW: A three-pestle mortar grinding snuff at Illingworth's Snuff Mill, founded in 1867 by an employee of Samuel Gawith.

ABOVE: A simple dog clutch and part of the gearing on a set of four single-pestle mortars – part of Thomas Harrison's original machinery and in use for two hundred years.

The snuffs made by the Kendal manufacturers have appeared under a variety of redolent brand names, such as Western Glory, Kendal Brown, Jockey Club, Carnation, After Glow, Otter Hound and Dr Rumney's Mentholyptus. Natural oils provide individual flavourings for snuff while chemical salts affect the colour and act as a preservative.

A. N. Middleton (ABOVE), a traditional miller, at his Sparkett Corn Mill. On the upper floor of the mill there are chutes for feeding the grain into the millstones.

At Little Salkeld, near Penrith, Nick Jones and his wife took over the old watermill and restored it to working life.

OPPOSITE, ABOVE: Nick Jones checks the consistency of the flour as it flows into a sack. The main gearing that drives the millstones can be clearly seen.

OPPOSITE, BELOW: Weighing wholemeal flour ready for distribution to Lakeland shops.

ABOVE: Parker Thompson 'gearing up'. He farms 90 acres with the help of four horses (mainly Shire, with some Clydesdale blood).

OPPOSITE, ABOVE: Parker Thompson ploughing in the traditional manner.

OPPOSITE, BELOW: Harrowing with two of the heavy horses, Royal and Anne, prior to sowing oats. Jack the dog follows behind.

LEFT: Harvey Bowe, from Braithwaite, near Keswick, has worked with horses for forty years. He uses a Clydesdale and (here) a Clydesdale crossed with a Felldale pony to cart timber for the Forestry Commission, in places which are too difficult for tractors. He remembers as many as ten horses being used for drawing timber even in the 1950s.

ABOVE: Bill Butler, a Flookburgh fisherman, offers his catch for sale at Kendal Market.

BELOW: Appleby Market, held every Saturday in Boroughgate, with stalls near the Moot Hall.

Mrs Betty Galloway using a stitch marker to punch small holes in her leather prior to stitching. On the table in front of her are some of the deerskin handicrafts she has produced, including flowers, handbags, belts and purses.

ABOVE: Flookburgh fishermen Albert Benson and Tommy Barker checking their nets in the Kent channel in Morecambe Bay. The rivers Leven and Kent pour into the bay gouging deep channels which change with the years sometimes quite dramatically. Generations of fishermen from the village of Flookburgh have negotiated the treacherous sands to catch the shrimps and fluke which are still a feature of the area today.

Flat fish, fluke or plaice, are caught with 'stream nets' staked out in the channel. As the tide flows in the net lifts up; on the ebb it stays down and the fish are trapped. The catch will also occasionally include cod, whiting or grey mullet. The fishermen go out to collect the fish and attend to their nets at each tide. Though fluke are taken throughout the year, the best months tend to be July and August. The shrimp fishermen do best in the autumn months, but March and April can also be good.

LEFT: The horse and cart has been replaced today by the tractor. In the heyday of an earlier generation of Flookburgh fishermen there were as many as thirty-two horses making their regular journeys out across the bay. It was not uncommon for the horses to get stuck in the quicksands, and not unknown for one to drown as the rapidly advancing tide swept up the bay. The tractors, too, have had their nasty moments. Albert Benson all but lost his when the vehicle stuck in a quicksand and was half submerged by the time other fishermen arrived to tow it out.

ABOVE: Brian Shaw has driven eight miles across Morecambe Bay from Flookburgh and is preparing his equipment to trawl for shrimps in the Kent channel. He uses two nets attached to the chassis of a London taxi, which is in turn tied to his tractor. The nets are trawled about five times per tide, the contents (BELOW) being emptied after each manoeuvre. The net size is determined by government regulations.

Back home from an afternoon's fishing in the bay, the fishermen prepare their catch for sale. Albert Benson is heading, gutting and washing fluke. Each shrimp fisherman, on the other hand, may employ as many as ten 'pickers' to remove the shrimp shells after each catch.

There are two kinds of crooks – those made entirely of wood and the crook which has a wooden shank and a ram's horn for the handle. The wood is usually hazel, readily available locally, though holly or blackthorn is also used. Once cut the sticks have to be seasoned for a minimum of two years and a periodic check is made to ensure they are straight. Some crook makers tie their shanks round a central thicker pole; Arthur Irvine (ABOVE) straightens his by bending them over his knee, using a little gentle heat if they prove reluctant. Here he is fitting a head of ram's horn on to the shank.

A crook made entirely of wood is selected for its straight shank and interesting root head. In the final preparation after the period of seasoning a saw may be used initially and then different surform files. A pocket knife is preferred to a chisel. The crook is finished with fine sandpaper and then varnished.

Arthur Irvine, a retired huntsman of the Eskdale and Ennerdale Foxhounds, looks for a round horn with plenty of thickness. He prefers Herdwick, but will also use Swaledale. The horn has to be rasped down and it is during this process that flaws may be revealed and the horn may have to be rejected. Heat is sometimes necessary to bend the horn finally to the desired shape; it is then secured by wire and held in a vice until cool. A hole is drilled into the head with a brace and bit to take the shank. Great care and skill are needed to ensure a tight fit. A ferrule may be added at the discretion of the craftsman.

Jim Wilson of Cockermouth, a well-known Lakeland craftsman, with some of his wooden crooks. This is Wasdale Show, the last show of the season, held in mid-October against the backcloth of Great Gable, Lingmell and Kirk Fell.

ABOVE: Mr and Mrs Joseph Fawcett of Glassonby.

BELOW: The rear of a cottage near Loweswater.

ABOVE: Stott Park Bobbin Mill, shortly before it closed. BELOW: Sam Rydal and Jim Graham at the saw bench.

OPPOSITE, ABOVE: Albert Graham, using the rincer, puts a hole through the birch blocks, ready for the roughing lathe.
OPPOSITE, BELOW: Wood shavings stream from a 'Fells' roughing lathe operated by Sam Rydal.
ABOVE: Sam Kellett operating a 100-year-old boring machine. All the machines in the lathe shed were belt driven via the overhead line shafting.

The bobbin industry flourished alongside the Lancashire cotton industry. A small cotton mill during the nineteenth century might have over 9,000 bobbins filling with cotton at any one time, and half the national requirement came from the Lakeland bobbin mills – nearly seventy in number, with High Furness and Staveley the centre of the industry. The cotton famine of the 1860s, combined with competition from Scandinavia, forced the bobbin makers to extend their range to additional products like brush, axe and spade handles, pill boxes and mangle rollers. The advent of the plastic bobbin was the final blow. Stott Park Mill, near Finsthwaite, survived until 1971.

When the water wheel became uneconomical, it was replaced by a Gilkes turbine – superseded in 1880 by this 10 h.p. single cylinder steam engine made in Brighouse.

OPPOSITE, ABOVE: Foreman Jim Graham at a hand finishing machine in the lathe shed. BELOW: George Dawson with a swill full of finished bobbins.

A 'sheep gather' at clipping time, Turner Hall Farm, Dunnerdale. Chris Hartley brings down part of the farm's flock of Herdwick sheep from the fells.

Herdwick wool made towns like Kendal and Ambleside prosperous in the sixteenth century, although while Kendal merchants grew fat on their profits, the land over the centuries became progressively poorer. The wool, if it has a fault, is coarse and rough to wear; it is, however, particularly warm. In this ultimate 'before and after' photograph (ABOVE), Bill Greenup (right) of Wasdale is wearing a suit made from Herdwick wool as he discusses the pros and cons of a Herdwick ewe with John Bowes of Broughton-in-Furness. The cloth was purchased from the Wool Marketing Board and made up by a local tailor.

OPPOSITE, ABOVE: Mrs Alice Holt, of Grange-over-Sands, engaged on her embroidery. She is a member of the Lakeland Guild of Local Craftsmen, who do much to encourage the pursuit of crafts and small industries.

OPPOSITE, BELOW: Surrounded by some typical Herdwick wool products, Miss M. E. Dalton crochets a hat.

ABOVE: Chris Reekie at his 100-year-old hand loom in the Grasmere workshop where he and his sons and grandsons weave rugs in a variety of natural colours.

OPPOSITE, ABOVE: A view of the spinning gallery at Yewtree Farm, on the road between Coniston and Ambleside. It can be reached by flights of stone steps from each end. There is a widely held view that these galleries were for storing and drying wool only, and indeed the galleries do occasionally have hooks in the roof, which would indicate that hanks of wool were hung there to dry; but there is little space for drying on a larger scale. A more romantic view is that the lady of the house sat spinning on the north side, where the light is good. One hopes in winter she was well wrapped in Herdwick.

LEFT: Mrs Cherry Morton of Clappersgate, near Ambleside, spinning outside her cottage. She first cards the cleaned wool (OPPOSITE, BELOW) to ensure the strands are parallel.

Neil Galloway of Threlkeld tying a broken thread before operating his power loom. He specialises in weaving Herdwick cloth for suit lengths and ties.

George Birkett shearing a ewe at Birk Howe Farm.

Cottages overlooking the green:
Askham, near Penrith.

Farmer Rupert Repton of Hampsfield Farm, near Cartmel.